Soul Ties

What's In Your Soul?

Tammy Henson

Published by Revival Waves of Glory Books & Publishing
PO Box 596| Litchfield, Illinois 62056 USA
www.revivalwavesofgloryministries.com

Revival Waves of Glory Books & Publishing is committed to excellence in the publishing industry.

EBook: 9783960280255
Paperback: 978-1-365-78813-0

Published in the United States of America

Table of Contents

Chapter 1
Opening Up Your Soul

Soul tie: a soul tie is a linkage in the spiritual realm between two people, who have been physically intimate with each other.

Let's look at key scripture:

Genesis 2:24

This is why a man leaves his father and mother and is united to his wife, and they become one flesh.

In this scripture we see, when a man leaves his parents and is united with a woman, they become one flesh. Therefore, their souls become one. What's in the mans soul enters the woman's soul and what's in the woman's soul enters the man's soul. God intended for it to be this way, but with married couples. [Premarital sex defiles the land] What happens a lot of times is what I like to call spiritual studies. [Sexually transmitted demons] This is why you can wake up the next morning, after intercourse feeling different. Having thoughts, feelings, or emotions you have never experienced before. You may feel like a different person. You may know someone who after intercourse changed. Sometimes their whole dynamics change. Maybe you're wondering what happened to them. It could be a soul tie. During intercourse you open yourself up to receive pleasure, therefore spiritual access is easy because your unguarded. Your soul is wide open and demons can enter. In the spirit realm you are giving permission to demons to enter. It is an open door, because you come into agreement with the enemy, and give him permission to enter.

There was a time in my life, I experienced this. I had been saved almost five years. I had previously gone through much deliverance. I made a mistake and had intercourse with a man. The next morning, my head was pounding and my stomach ached. [It was in a lot of pain] Instantly at that moment, I realized what had just happened. [During the events the enemy had me blinded] I made an agreement with the enemy. I was fully loaded with demons. [The man wasn't saved and into a lot of sin] What was in his soul was now tied to my soul. I had to battle things that I never thought I'd have to battle again. I had to fight my way back. That sin separated me from God, which is what hurt me the most. For several months I had to be delivered of all the junk I gave permission to enter. [I felt it come out of my nose, ears, and mouth; it tasted horrible] Usually when we aren't saved you don't feel what I felt. It does not mean we don't make an exchange of demons during intercourse. It just means most unsaved people already have demons, so when the exchange occurs, it's not noticeable.

Let's look at key scripture

Isaiah 59:2

Sin separates you from God.

In my experience God taught me something. He taught me why I was separated from him. It was because there were demons at work. Light cannot shine in darkness. He taught me our connection was being blocked and hindered by dark forces. The more I fought and the more I was delivered, the more presence and light I could feel. Therefore the more ground I took back from the enemy, the more I received from heaven.

Let's look at another key scripture

2 Corinthians 6:14

Do not be unequally yoked together with unbelievers. For what do Righteousness and wickedness have in common? Or what fellowship can light have with darkness?

In this scripture, we see that being in any form of relationship or fellowship with anyone who isn't like minded, comes with consequences. It takes for a bumpy road with uncommon ground. If you were walking down the road on a sunny day and someone invited you to walk down a dark and dreary alley, would you go? We must obey God in this. We open ourselves up to the spiritual climate around us, and our soul soaks it in.

Let's look at another key scripture

Amos 3:3

Can two walk together unless they agree?

Here we see, to walk with someone, you must be in agreement. What are you in agreement with??? What and who are you walking with? You are literally giving permission to these things to abide with you. Sometimes we create our own problems, by giving written permission to outside forces!

Let's look at key scripture

1 Corinthians 6:18

Flee fornication, every sin that a man does is without the body, but he that commits fornication sins against his own body.

In this scripture we see that fornication, causes you to sin against your own body. When you are involved in the sin of fornication, you create a soul tie. You open yourself up to it. You are in agreement with the enemy. In the spiritual realm you are saying the enemy has permission, to connect someone else's soul to yours. What are you opening your soul up to? We must pay attention to what people look like in the spirit. It might not be too pretty in there. It matters greatly who we open ourselves up to!

Chapter 2
Viewing the Soul Tie

There are things to watch for, in others and in yourself. Let's take a look at what these things are.

-Obsessive involvement with another

-Displays domineering behavior and controlling in a relationship

-Displays passive behavior and apathy in a relationship [easily manipulated]

-Hard to truly forgive

-Hearing someone else's voice playing over and over in your head

-Difficult to bring a relationship to godly order and control of the Holy Spirit

-Displays behavior of anger, blames, and accusations in a relationship

-Fear of speaking truth to another

-Psychic or occult phenomena in a relationship

Do you suffer from a broken heart? Can you not get someone out of your mind? Can you see them and hear them in your head? Do they display any of these characteristics? You could have a soul tie!

Let's look at key scripture

Genesis 34 2-3

And when Shechem the son of Hamor the Hivite, prince of the country, saw her then took her and laid with her and defiled her. And his soul cleaved unto Dinah the daughters of Jacob, and he loved the damsel and spoke kindly to the damsel.

In this scripture we see when he lay with her his soul cleaved to her, therefore forming a soul tie.

God intended for a man and a woman to marry before intercourse. When we have intercourse before marriage, it causes defilement.

Defilement is defined; to make unclean or impure, to make physically unclean, especially with something unpleasant or contaminating, or to violate the sanctity. [Merriam-Webster dictionary]

Let's look at key scripture

1 Corinthians 7:2

Nevertheless, to avoid fornication, let every man have his own wife and every woman have her own husband.

We see here it I a sin to have intercourse outside of marriage.

Let's look at key scripture

Hebrews 13:4

Marriage is honorable in all, and the bed undefiled: but the whoremongers, and adulterers God will judge

You see, sin defiles the land. Intercourse connects us to another persons soul. A soul tie is formed even with those who marry, but those who are unwed also open up the door to defilement.

To take a deeper look at this let's examine and look at these stories

Story#1: Tom and Lisa are married. They waited to have intercourse till their wedding day. They made their vows and are committed to each other. They have formed a soul tie. A soul tie God intended for married couples to have. Tom drinks and struggles with anger. He is controlling and blames Lisa for things. Lisa is passive and does whatever she can to keep her husband happy and smiling. Before they were married Lisa felt good about herself, she was assertive, and had boundaries. After the wedding day and the soul tie; his soul wounded her. She became somewhat different. Even though the defilement wasn't part of their story, the soul tie was.

Story#2: Bob and Kathy are not married, but see each other regularly. They are having intercourse with each other. They have a lot in common. They both love the arts, they both love wine, they both love western and war movies, and many other things. They both work and are somewhat responsible, but they are blinded by the enemy on the defects. They see only the good. They see through these rose colored glasses. A spirit of ignorance is upon them both. They have a soul tie, which has brought them under the enemy's control. But sin defiles the land. The defilement opened up the door to the blinding and ignorance. It also opens the door to witchcraft control.

Let's look at key scripture

Lamentations 4:14

They have wandered as blind men in the streets, they have polluted themselves with blood, so that men could not touch their garments.

We see here because of their sin, they wandered around blindly. They polluted themselves because of the spiritually unclean blood. No touch… garments- as being defiled with blood. Blood here means lust or the sin of lust/perversity. [My personal revelation to me]

Also defilement is a direct open door to the enemy to attack you with different spirits. Where as a married couple that door is closed.

Chapter 3
Codependency and the Soul Tie

Codependency: excessive emotional or psychological reliance on a partner.

Let's look at key scripture

Galatians 1:10

For am I seeking the approval of man or of god? Or am I trying to please man? If I were still trying to please man, I wouldn't be a servant of Christ.

We see here you can not please God and man. Seeking to please man causes dysfunction of various types. It wounds your soul. It's a sin and an open door.

Let's look at key scripture

1 Thessalonians 2:4

But just as we have been approved by God, to be entrusted with the gospel, so we speak, not to please man, but to please God who tests our hearts.

Here we see we should speak to please god not man. Many in codependency seek to please others. They walk on egg shells around them. They don't want anyone mad at them. They thrive off approval from others, and they live in fear of confrontation. This is an open door to anxiety and many other things. Can you see how one thing leads to another? One open door leads to another open door. Codependent persons get their value and worth from others. Never knowing who they really are. [Forming a soul tie]

Let's look at key scripture

Proverbs 29:25

The fear of man brings a snare, but whoever trusts in the Lord shall be safe.

Here we see being in fear of others or depend on others will bring a snare, or a net to catch you in; to trap and entangle you with some sort of bondage.

Let's look at key scripture

Proverbs 8:36

But he who sins against me wrongs his own soul; all those who hate me love death.

Here we see sin causes sin causes you to wrong your own soul. To wound it, to cause sickness to come to it. "Infliction" we also see, that's why God says to obey him. Gods not hard or mean. He is only trying to protect us. This verse goes on to further say, those who hate me love death, because the result of sin is death. Sometimes spiritual death and sometimes physical death. The bible states if we love God, we will obey him. [John 14:15] Therefore, if we don't obey him, we hate him, and love the result of sin which is death.

Are you codependent? Are you unable to find satisfaction without someone else? Do you recognize unhealthy behaviors in your partner? But stay anyways! Are you giving support to your partner at the cost of your own mental, emotional, or physical health? Are you engulfed in a relationship despite the negative consequences? You can become burned out and exhausted. You can ignore other important relationships! You can ignore your own needs and identify and meet the needs of someone else, and there's major consequences. This could be the result of a soul tie. Codependency is also the pattern of painful dependence on compulsive behaviors. In an attempt to find safety, self worth, and identity.

Symptoms of codependency

-Intense and unstable interpersonal relationships

-Inability to tolerate being alone, accompanied by efforts to avoid it

-Chronic feelings of boredom and emptiness

-Putting off your needs of someone else

-Overwhelming desire for acceptance and affection

-Dishonesty

-Denial

-Low self worth

Behaviors of codependency

-Focused on others

-Excessive complaint

-Self sacrificing

-Reactive

-Problems opening up to intimacy

-Controlling

-Manipulative

The enemy lies… he has you thinking your gaining worth and value and also identity. But the truth is, your giving it away. You conform to fit who others are, never meeting who you are.

Let's look at a beautiful verse on who we are

Psalm 139:14

I praise you, for I am fearfully and wonderfully made. Wonderful are your works, my soul knows it very well.

Here we see who we are. We are fearfully made. [Unique and with great reverence, with heartfelt interest and respect] We are wonderfully made [bright, special, honored and adored] wonderful are your works. [Indicates God worked to create a beautiful work of art, that is the reflection in the mirror. When you look at it and it's you.] and my soul knows it well. [your soul is your thoughts, your desires, and your feelings.] so your soul knows who you are and knows your identity. So next time you look in the mirror, tell the person looking at you that you are fearfully and wonderfully made.

Chapter 4

Transference of Spirits and the Soul Ties

As I have previously said, as a soul tie is formed there can be a transference of spirits. In chapter one I stated that when a man and woman unite or have relations their souls connect and become one. What's in the man's soul enters the woman's soul and what's in the woman's soul enters the man's soul. Therefore, trading or exchanging spirits. The enemy's favorite tool is to get people in bondage and take over their minds, their wills, and their emotions. Soul ties can be formed in other ways [which we will briefly discuss later] but intercourse is the enemy's favorite weapon. It's easy and productive. Let's take a look at this in secular and spiritual terms. When two people have intercourse; there's two responses taking place. In the natural it feels good, it feels right, and the intimacy is amazing. The kissing and the hugging. In the spiritual realm you are unguarded. You open yourself up to receive pleasure in the natural, so the spiritual side has full access to attack. You open yourself up to demons. They will implant themselves in your soul. You know why? Because they have a legal right.

Demons are all about law and rights. They will use even the smallest excuse. That's why it's so important to be married before intercourse.

Exchange: Is to give and receive in return or to trade.

I recently read an article on hugging one another [spiritual research foundation] It was very interesting. The study indicated that even through a hug, we exchange energy. Kissing transfers more energy than a hug. It indicated that people are affected by negative energy. When the bible talks about demons, a lot of the time it refers to them as the power of the air. Hmm, interesting. Isn't that energy.

Let's look at key scripture

Proverbs 4:23

Keep your heart with all diligence, for out of it flows the issues of life.

God spoke to me and he said an unguarded heart [soul] is access opened up. Exchange, what are we exchanging?

Through prayer and a little study, this is what I found.

-When two people touch there is a friction caused when their mental coverings connect. This usually creates distressing vibrations which can be taken advantage of by negative energies to affect the people involved.

-Even with minimal contact such as a hug who practicing spirituality can be affected by black energy. This causes distress to persons on separate paths of devotion to a God that's not Jesus.

-Hugging mentally ill patients will have an adverse spiritual affect for the person hugging. Mentally ill patients have a high likelihood of being affected by negative feelings.

-Even children, especially when hugging parents can feel and pick up on negative energies.

Things to keep in mind

-Make sure you only touch or hug those you're close to, limit hugging don't just hug or touch anyone, you don't know what their negative energies are.

-Practice regular time with God, to provide a protective covering.

-Prayer defeats negative energies

Let's look at key scripture

Ephesians 2:2

In which you used to walk according to this world, according to the power of the air; the spirit that is now working in the sons of disobedience.

Disobedience causes the enemy to grip you and those negative energies belong to the power of the air, which is Satan.

Have you ever wondered why someone can seem to get into relationships with the same kind of people. A woman seems to draw in alcoholics and/or abusers. Its in the negative energies. Like a magnet its an attraction to most unknown. A spiritual attraction manifesting in the natural. Also spirits attract each other.

Story; Amy grew up in a small town. Her mom was a stay at home mom, and her dad was an alcoholic who worked a lot. He was at work for thirty days and home for thirty days. Her mom started drinking out of loneliness and became an alcohol as well. Amy grew up with the spirit of alcohol. She never drank because she has seen the effects it had on her siblings and her parents, but she had this on her spirit. So it drew alcoholics to her, because she grew up with it and carried that spirit with her. It was like a magnet that drew other alcoholics to her.

Let's look at key scripture

Proverbs 12:26

The righteous should choose his friends carefully, for the way of the wicked leads them astray

We see here the ways of the wicked lead us astray why? Because it's a spirit. The spirit causes negative energy that can hinder or lead you astray.

Let's look at key scripture

Psalms1:1

Blessed is the man who walks not in the counsel of the ungodly, nor stands in the paths of sinners, nor sits in the seat of the scornful

We see here that staying away from the ungodly causes you to be blessed. Blessed means happy and highly favored. So walking with sinners or the scornful, in comparison to being blessed would be cursed. It is my belief that God wanted us not to associate with the ungodly and be around their wickedness because of their negative energy. which we have discovered comes from the power of the air, satan and his minions. Therefore causing the transference of spirits and soul ties.

In closing this chapter I wanted to add; that I have encountered many spirits. I have come into contact with them through various forms of contact. Through intercourse, through ungodly friendships, and also through a hug at Walmart passing by an old friend. This is a spiritual world we live in and is invisible to the natural eye. There's obvious reasons to me why God says no, and it's because he loves you and wants the best for you.

Let's look at key scripture

Ephesians 6:12

For we do not wrestle against flesh, in blood, but against rulers, against the authorities, against the powers of darkness, against the spiritual forces of evil in heavenly places.

You see it's our enemy we are fighting and he will do what he can to attack, its legal access. So obey God and move into the shelter of the Lord God Almighty.

When you walk into a church you carry a spirit with you. Tuning into it, you can pick it up. By transferring it to them.

Causes positive and negative

-Laying on of hands

-Word or communication

*regular time with unbelievers causes corrupt behavior and transfers spirits via association

-via association

*transferred spirits are easily introduced, its strongly advised to not be unequally yoked for this reason

-Intercourse

*easiest way and most powerful unholy soul ties

- via parents

*transferred to children, almost always, goes from one generation to the next

-music

*powerful evil spirits transferred through immorality, violence, and worshipping demons

-Food-water-drinks

*communion -good holy spirits

*occult practices-unholy evil spirits

- Objects and materials

   *statues, movies, books, necklaces, cloths

-Reincarnation

   *practices, rituals, worship

-Dead and burial ceremonies

   *people possessed by demons when they die an evil spirit doesn't, the spirits look quickly for another prey

Chapter 5

Ties That Bind

Let's take a look at a deeper level of things.

Let's look at key scripture

Romans 12:2

Do not conform to the pattern of this world, but be transformed by the renewing of your mind. Then you will be able to test and approve what Gods will is, his pleasing and perfect will.

To transform is to completely change from one thing to another and the way to transform is to renew your mind. To renew your mind is to make like new, or restore to freshness. To do this we must fill our minds with godly things and turn away from ungodly things.

There are things that open us up to allow things into our souls. Whatever is connected to these ungodly things enters our soul and becomes one with us.

Let's examine them.

-music

-gossip

-the occult

-drugs and alcohol

-worshipping other gods

-anger

There are more things that open our souls up and allow demons to enter. This is just a short list of what I believe to be important.

Let's begin by discussing music. We have godly music and we have ungodly music. We also have music that isn't either one. There's not much of it out there, but none the less it is there. The music we listen to matters. It is the spirit behind what we listen to. We make an agreement in the spiritual realm and accept these spirits into our souls as we listen to them. Much [not all] rock music has a Satanism spirit, witchcraft, division, sorcery, and hatred/violence. There's a quote in it and its "do what you want, be rebellious, and break the law" So when you make an agreement with rock music [not all] this is what you are accepting in your soul. To be part of who you are. There's spirits behind rap music. [not all] The spirit of Jezebel, the spirit of lust, seduction, immorality, the spirit of control, fear, denial, and blame. Some also have leviathan and this is the spirit behind drugs and violent crimes. There's spirits behind country music [not all] Self pity, depression, passiveness, seduction, oppression, death, addiction and laziness. These are just the main three types of music. I didn't list them all or list all the spirits behind the music. Just the main important ones.

Let's look at key scripture

Proverbs 28:4

Those that forsake the law, praise the wicked, but those who keep the law strive with them.

We see here that those who forsake or abandon the ways of the lord, praise wickedness. To praise is to admire or approve. But those who keep the law strive or go to great lengths to be part of it.

What's in the music you're listening to? What are you praising?

Let's look at key scripture

Luke 6:45

A good man brings good things out of the good stored up in his heart, and an evil man brings evil things out of the evil stored up in his heart. For the mouth speaks what the heart is full of.

We see here the words that come forth from a person are out of the things stored in his heart. [heart issues] The heart of a man is his soul. So whomever you listen to in the music you make a soul tie with their soul. [Who is singing the music? What is in their heart? What are they transferring to you?] and accept their demons into your soul. So again, I ask what's behind the music you are listening to?

Lets discuss gossip. It's a sin. Many people struggle with this. Why is it such a sin? First, it ruins another's reputation. Second, it opens us up to spirits. When we gossip about someone it gives the enemy permission to attack them and you, and it wreaks havoc on people's lives.

Story#1 Barb was praying one morning, she was having a hard time forgiving her mother. She has a long history of pain and anger. One day God tells her as a child she randomly spoke against her own deliverance. God reminds her of things she said. "I will never forgive her" I will turn my back on her when I'm old enough" and "I hate you" well no wonder she was having such a problem letting things go and forgiving. She word cursed the relationship and she needed to ask forgiveness and cancel every word curse. What the enemy did was, took her words and create what she spoke. He attacked both of them.

Story# 2 Tanya got her children taken. She had been on drugs and couldn't control her use. During a battle to get them back, the people who had them didn't want to give them back. So the people lied and said she abused them. A case was opened, people looked at her funny, talked about her, and ridiculed her. She never got her kids back and this devastated her. Talk about ruining a reputation. Today she is saved and fighting for her children daily.

Story #3 Ted and his sister Connie are six years apart, he was always jealous of her, and felt rejected. He suffered mentally by perceived rejection and some actual rejection as well. He told Connie growing up, he couldn't wait to get away from her when he grew up. He told her they weren't ever going to talk and he hated her. Today they live across town from each other and they rarely speak. It's uncomfortable when they do and they don't like each other. Connie thinks of the painful experiences growing up with him and resents him. Ted wonders why Connie is the way she is. He just wants his sister to have a relationship with him. Here we see Ted's words created a reality, and the enemy attacked the relationship.

Proverbs 18:21

Death and life are in the power of the tongue, those who love it will eat its fruits.

We see here that what we speak becomes the fruit of our reality. Words have power and words create either life or death. Good or evil.

What are you speaking?

Let's look at key scripture

Proverbs 29:5

Whoever flatters his neighbor spreads a net for his feet

Here we see that whoever flatters which means to speak ill of sets a net for the other person's feet. This is a good example of satan attacking someone as a result of the words of our mouth.

Let's look at key scripture

Proverbs 26:28

A lying tongue hates those who are crushed by it and a flattering mouth works ruin.

We see here that people are crushed by lies against them, and a person who flatters with their mouth is working to ruin others.

What does God say about the sin of gossip?

Let's look at key scripture

Proverbs 6:12-15

A worthless person, a wicked man, walks with a perverse mouth; he winks with eyes, he shuffles his feet, he points with his fingers; perversity is in his heart. He devises evil continually, he sows discord, therefore his calamity shall come suddenly, he shall be broken without remedy.

WOW… what a consequence of the sin of gossip. Here we see the characteristics of a wicked and perverse person. We see his intent and furthermore see that sudden calamity is the cause. The word also gives demonstration of this in Galatians 6:7 when it says be not deceived, God is not mocked for what a man sows he shall reap. So next time you feel tempted to gossip think about what you are doing, and never join in with others while they are gossiping.

Let's talk about the occult. What is the occult? The dictionary describes it as supernatural, mystical or magical powers [dictionary.com] Examples of occult practices are magic [black or white] sorcery, Ouija boards, tarot cards, Satanism, fortune telling, witchcraft [Wicca] and practices of astrology. Occult practices appeal to the natural mind. Many people dabble in it out of curiosity and see it as harmless. But you see yourself going deeper and deeper. Being in or participating in the occult is dangerous. There are characteristics to look for or be aware of for those in the occult.

-False prophets

-They seek to influence other people, particularly those in leadership

-They try to hinder the true gospel from being preached

[We are to be alert and self-controlled against the schemes of the enemy]

Let's look at key scripture

Leviticus 19:31

Do not turn to mediums or necromancers, do not seek them out, for by doing so, you make yourself unclean, I am the lord your God.

We see here God warns against seeking mediums or fortune tellers. Why? Because it causes you to become unclean. What exactly does that mean. It means you open up your soul to the spirits in the occult. You tie your soul to the bondages and powers of the occult. [torments]

Let's look at key scripture

Ezekiel 13:18

Thus says the Lord, woe to the woman who sew magic bonds upon all wrists and make veils for the heads of persons of every statue in the hunt for souls. Will you hunt down souls belonging to my people? And keep your own souls alive.

We see those here who are in the occult or use magic to grip their victims for their benefit ruins their soul, it inflicts torture and pain and removes peace and comfort. It brings destruction and inflicts their soul with evil spirits. So God is saying will you keep your own soul alive? Because destruction will come for yours. These things are not innocent or games to play. They bring real consequences and torments to our souls. They can control and take over your life.

There was a time in my own life I was in the full grip of satan and being controlled and tormented by his hosts. I know what its like and its death and witchcrafts entangle and choke you out.

Let's look at key scripture

Acts 16:16

As we were going to a place of prayer, we were met by a slave girl who had a spirit of divination and brought her owners much gain by fortune telling.

We see her this girl had a spirit in her soul. She had a spirit of divination. She had power that was evil, and it was a spirit behind the occult practices.

Let's talk about drugs and alcohol. There are many different types of drugs and many different types of alcohol. Just like music, gossip, and the occult; there's consequences. There are spirits connected to drugs and alcohol. Many times this is the reason why people try to quit and can't. This also goes for cigarettes, there's a spirit of nicotine that grabs a hold of you and you have to battle these spirits. Unless God supernaturally sets you free. Let's focus on alcohol for a moment. In small doses its been said its healthy for stimulation of the heart and body. But in large doses also known as heavy drinking, it affects the brain, heart, liver, and pancreas. Causing a person to be more prone to cancer and illness due to a weak immune system. When drinking excessively your unguarded and spirits can take advantage. Alcohol draws in negative vibrations and can easily enter your soul while intoxicated, because intoxication reduces the ability to sense those negative energies we previously discussed. Therefore, making an unconscious agreement with the enemy to enter your soul. It is my belief that Jesus wasn't against drinking. He turned the water into wine. [John 2:1-11] but he warned against being a drunkard.

Let's look at key scripture

Ephesians 5:18-21

And be not drunk with wine, in excess, but be filled with the spirit, speaking to yourselves in psalms and hymns and spiritual songs, singing and making melody in your heart to the lord; giving thanks always for all things unto God and the father in the name of our lord Jesus Christ, submitting to one another in the fear of the lord.

Here we see God says not to be drunk he does not say don't drink. He says not to be drunk with wine, in excess [over consumption, more than necessary, or overindulgence] but be filled with the spirit, he goes on to say to speak and sing in songs. Why? Because excessive alcohol use causes depression not singing. It takes root in your heart. Excessive drinking causes a sad heart not a melody in your heart [gratitude] and that's why scripture says "make melody in your heart" He says give thanks always. Why? Because excessive drinking or being a drunkard causes you to be unthankful and bitter. He further says to submit to one another in the fear of the lord. Why? Drunkards become selfish and only fear themselves, and only submit to themselves. All spirits that we accept into our souls.

Let's look at key scripture

Proverbs 23 :29-35

Who has woe? Who has sorrow? Who has contentions? Who has complaints? Who has wounds without a cause? Who has redness of eyes? Those who linger long at the wine. Those who go in search of mixed wine. Do not look on the wine when it is red, when it sparkles in your cup, when it swirls round smoothly. At the last it bites like a serpent and stings like a viper. Your eyes will see strange things, and your heart will utter perverse things. Yeah, you will be like one who lies down in the midst of the sea or like one who lies at the top or the mast, saying ' they have stuck me, but I was not hurt, they have beaten me but I did not feel it. When shall I awake that I may seek another drink.

Here we see in the beginning everything we experience as being intoxicated or a drunkard. It goes on to say at the last it bites like a serpent and stings like a viper. Its saying the end result is death. It is also saying a spirit of python [to choke and kill] is involved and a viper to inject venom or poison in you. Your eyes will see strange things it says. It brings delusions and confusion. It says your heart [soul] will utter perverse things. You accept the spirit of perversity into your soul. It also says you will be like the one who lays down in the midst of the sea. Here we see leviathan. The spirit of leviathan is the creature of the sea. Then it says you struck me and beat me and I didn't feel it. Why? Because I was drunk and numb. When your drunk your emotions are frozen solid and you don't feel pain. Then it says when shall I awake in seeking another drink? Because when the numbness and tingling go away and you sober up the pain returns and it hurts tremendously.

Let's look at scripture on leviathan/python

Amos 9:3

And though they hide themselves in the top of Carmel [top of the mast] I will search and take them out, and though they hide from my sight in the bottom of the sea, I will command the serpent and he shall bite them.

Here we see that we try to hide ourselves in our drunkard state, but we are only hidden in the nets or traps of leviathan and the painful bites of the serpent/snakes.

Let's look at key scripture on leviathan

Psalm 104:26

There the ships sail about, there is that leviathan which you have made to play there.

Here we see you have made leviathan your playmate.

I would like to add that alcohol and drugs are one in the same. The bible talks about drunkards and also refers to it as intoxicated. Which means drugs and alcohol. It is all substances that lead to intoxication. It all leads to the same place. The cause and effect are the same, and there are spirits connected to both.

There was a time in my life I was addicted to drugs. For 10 plus years. I wanted to quit and couldn't. It ruined my life and stole everything from me. [the enemy comes to steal, kill, and destroy] Jesus found me right in time and I gave my life to him. For the first year I struggled with drugs. I know what it's like to fight for your life. These spirits weren't just going to leave. I was in a spiritual battle and it was truly a fight. The truth does set you free. Through it all God taught me how to fight and how to trust him as my healer. He also taught me the truth behind what was really going on. Through experience every time I got high again he showed me something else. This is the truth that sets me free. I was set free from demonic powers that gripped me for years. All the glory goes to Jesus. My lord and savior. The lover of my soul. Thank you JESUS.

Let's talk about worshipping other gods. The god you serve also comes with a spirit. In Christianity the spirit we receive is the holy spirit. The Holy Spirit has character traits and they are, love, joy, peace, long-suffering, kindness, goodness, faithfulness, gentleness, and self-control.

Let's look at key scripture

Galatians 5:22-23

But the fruit of the spirit is love, joy, peace, long suffering, kindness, goodness, faithfulness, gentleness, and self-control.

We see here who god clearly is. [Jesus]

Let's look at key scripture

1 Corinthians 10:20

No, I imply what pagans sacrifice they offer to demons and not to God. I do not want you to be participants with demons.

Here we see that pagans are worshipping demons and open their souls to demons through spiritual doorways. They make agreements and establish demonic connections.

Let's look at key scripture

Psalm135:15-18

The idols of the nations are silver and gold, the work of human hands. They have mouths, but do not speak, they have eyes but do not see, they have ears, but do not hear, nor is there any breath in their mouths. Those who make them become like them, so do all who trust in them.

Here we see that idols or other gods have mouths, but speak evil, they have eyes, but only see what they want to see, they have ears but only hear demons. There's no breath in their mouths; meaning there's no life in them. Those who serve them make them or trust them because they're just like them.

Let's look at key scripture

Colossians 3:5

Put to death what is earthly in you. Sexual immorality, impurity, passion, evil desire, and covetousness which is idolatry.

Here we see all these things are character traits of other gods. We open our souls up to these things. Therefore giving demons legal access to our souls, by sinning and worshipping other gods.

As a follower of Jesus, we may worship things above god. Money? Possessions? Social media? , movies? The list can go on. Some worship other gods like Islam, Buddhism, and Hinduism. The list can go on. The question is what are you allowing into your soul? What's tied to your soul? God says no to things because it harms us. Why does it harm us? Because it welcomes demons into our souls? It takes residence as you are their new home. You take on the characteristics of what is tied to your soul.

Let's look at key scripture

Matthew 12:29

How can one enter a strong man's house and plunder his goods, unless he first binds the strongman and then he will plunder his house.

We see here that in order to get free you have to bind the strongman and cast him out. Then you can plunder his house and have it given back to you. You see we have given our souls to demons by various acts and behaviors. Which means we no longer own ourselves. The good news is there's power in the blood of Jesus. To break this off our lives. This is why deliverance is so important. When we give our heart to Jesus we are saved, but our souls are full of junk. Jesus died so we could be set free. It's by his stripes we are healed. It doesn't happen overnight, but he is our redeemer. It's a spiritual battle, and we overcome by the blood of the lamb and the word of our testimony.

Let's talk about anger. Anger is a strong feeling of displeasure caused by a wrong. Anger us a natural emotion.

Let's look at key scripture

Ephesians 4: 26-27

When angry do not sin. Don't let the sun go down on your wrath, nor give place to the devil.

We see ere that it's okay to get angry. It's what we do with that anger that matters. We should let all things go before the sun goes down. Why? Because it opens the door for a foothold. It gives place to the devil. We open up our soul to the enemy when we behave irrationally out of anger. Human anger does not produce the righteousness that God desires. [James 1:20]

Let's look at key scripture

Psalms 4:4

Tremble and do not sin, when you are on your beds searching your hearts and be silent.

Here we see the resolution or the resolve. God is saying before you go to bed search your hearts, in other words quietly release anger or the negative from the day out of your soul. Be quiet before him and let his spirit guide to the way to humility and forgiveness.

What then are the results of anger. Why is it such a sin to act out in anger. What are the open doors?

Let's look at key scripture

Proverbs 29:22

A man of wrath stirs up strife, and one given to anger causes much transgression.

LOOK... here we see anger causes wrath and strife. Its consequences are transgression. What is a transgression? It is a fault, offense, crime, sin, violation of law or overstepping a boundary or limit. [Merriam dictionary] Sin and transgression open our souls up to the demonic. Disobeying god is serious business. There's consequences to our actions.

Let's look at key scripture

James 1:15

Then, after desire has conceived, it gives birth to sin. When its full grown it gives birth to death.

Here we see we give place to the spirit of death. Death is ruin and destruction. So we open our souls up to destruction and ruin. To darkness and death. Everything about us dies. The enemy takes full advantage and disassembles life and light. Joy and happiness. Anger is only one piece of the pie. One of the many sins that invite demons into your soul and are tied to them.

Chapter 6

Good Soul Ties

Let's talk about good soul ties. God created soul ties. Satan counterfeits them. It is a help to man if it's a healthy soul tie created by God.

Let's look at key scripture

Genesis 2:20-22

Adam gave names to all cattle, and the foul of the air and every beast of the field, but there was no helper for him. And the Lord caused Adam to fall into a deep sleep and took one of his ribs and closed up his flesh. And the rib which god took he made woman and brought her to the man.

We see here Eve was made to be a helper to Adam. To come into the garden with Adam as one. To make a soul tie to become one and help each other. To reflect each other and to strengthen each other.

Let's look at key scripture

Samuel 18:1

And it came to pass, when he had made an end of speaking unto Saul, that the soul of Jonathan was knit to the soul of David. And Jonathan loved him as his own soul.

We see here Jonathan and David had a soul tie. Their souls were knitted together. And Jonathan loved him as his own soul. The purpose of soul ties created by God is to care for another person deeply. To come together as one with compassion and help each other with a Godly love.

There's a connection or an exchange in Godly soul ties as well. [married couples] It creates a strong foundation. Its purpose is to build up and feed each other. It's like a strong tower. Two people linked together make it taller, stronger, and wider. It's a shelter and a safety. It's a pulling rod to have on your side. It's like rock climbing something to guard you and cover you.

Let's look at key scripture

Mark 10:9

Therefore what God has joined together, let no man separate.

We see here that what God joins together, it is difficult to separate because its strong and built up.

It's bonded together and can't be broken.

Let's look at key scripture

Proverbs 18:10

The name of the Lord is a strong tower, the righteous run to it and are safe.

We see here that God is the creator of marriage. He is the one who is head of it. It's created in his name and forms as a strong tower. Married couples run to it and are safe.

Soul Tie Prayer

Lord Jesus, I come before you and I kneel in surrender to your Holy Throne. I ask forgiveness for any fornication, or ungodly sexual acts. Forgive me of the sins of anger, unholy demonic music, gossip, judgement, worshipping other gods, occult practices, drugs or alcohol. Knowingly or unknowingly. Remove the ties that bind demons to my soul. I cancel every agreement with the enemy and call it canceled null and void. I remove every legal right and cast it down. Lord cleanse me from every evil spirit and every bondage of hell. Restore my soul and refresh it. Make me whole. I cancel every unholy word or vow. Forgive me, Lord. I call every piece of my soul back to me and I give back every piece to anyone or anything that doesn't belong to me. Thank you Jesus for your cleansing rains and the power of your blood and resurrection. I apply Dunamis power to my soul and call it whole. In the name of my Lord and Savior Jesus Christ.

Other books available By Tammy Henson

Cries of the Soul Volume 1

Cries of the Soul Volume 2

Deep Roots of the Soul

Cries of the Soul Complete Edition